# TAMIEKA LEE

# THE WORLD IS
# YOURS

A Foundational Guide to Reaching Goal Success

*The World is Yours: A Foundational Guide to Reaching Goal Success*

Copyright © 2020 by Tamieka Lee. All rights reserved.

No part of this book may be used or reproduced in any manner whatsoever without written permission, except in the case of brief quotations embodied in critical articles or reviews.

Scripture quotations from the King James Version (KJV) unless stated otherwise.

Scripture quotations marked (ESV) are from the ESV® Bible (The Holy Bible, English Standard Version®), copyright © 2001 by Crossway, a publishing ministry of Good News Publishers. Used by permission. All rights reserved.

**Editing and Interior Design**
DHBonner Virtual Solutions, LLC
www.dhbonner.net

**Cover Design**
Elonzo Coleman – Liquidstyle Design Studio
www.liquidstyleds.com

**Photograph for Cover Design**
Anthony Green Photography
www.vimeo.com/anthonytgreen

**Photograph Cover Design Studio**
Sophia Gilmore | Sophia's Professional Photography

ISBN: 978-0-578-65884-1

Printed in The United States of America

# TABLE OF CONTENTS

| | |
|---|---|
| *Acknowledgments* | v |
| *Introduction* | ix |
| 1. The Importance of Persistence | 1 |
| 2. Original Individual | 9 |
| 3. Make Light out of Your Vision | 15 |
| 4. Your Mind is a Terrible Thing to Waste | 19 |
| 5. More Discipline, Much Closer | 25 |
| 6. Are you Consistent Enough? | 31 |
| 7. You Must Learn | 37 |
| 8. Unswerving Determination | 45 |
| 9. Iron Sharpens Iron | 51 |
| 10. Challenging You | 59 |
| 11. Keep Ya Head Up | 65 |
| 12. Work Your Prayers and Faith | 73 |
| *About the Author* | 81 |
| *Notes* | 83 |
| *Additional Reading* | 85 |

ACKNOWLEDGMENTS

Allow me to start by giving thanks to my Lord and Savior, Jesus Christ. He is the Master of my life and my Source of inspiration for this project. God provided strength through His Word, guidance by way of revelation, and the vision of me reaching people in a way that is now manifested in the form of this book. All glory, honor, and praise to You for ordering my steps along this path of purpose! Father God, I pray that *The World is Yours* reaches the multitudes that You have called me to impact. May every page bless the reader by the power of Your anointing. Amen.

To my mother and brother, Yuma and Renardo Lee . . . I appreciate you both for always believing in me. Your unwavering support, through every life decision, has been the anchor that enables me to remain steadfast in my pursuit of destiny. Know that your love for me is an irreplaceable constant in my world. I love you two! Thank you for encouraging me to keep the faith and driving me further towards the things of God. Broski, we have endured much, BUT GOD! Yuma Jean, your memory lives on through me. You are truly missed. I thank God for assigning you and Renardo Carson as my parents. May you both rest in heaven until we meet again.

I would be remiss not to thank my spiritual family. If it had not been for your commitment to imparting the knowledge of God, I would not have received the gift of eternal salvation. Bishop Keith A. Butler and Pastor Debra Butler, Pastor Andre Butler and Minister Tiffany Butler, Pastors Lee Ferguson and Michelle Butler-Ferguson, Pastor Joel Jenkins and Ministers Kristina Butler-Jenkins, as well as all of the spiritual leaders who have contributed to my growth, thanks for your dedication to delivering the Word of God for the advancement of His kingdom. I am a virtuous woman as a result of your influence. Thank you.

Mr. Nasir Jones, you are both a legend and a change agent! You inspired my title, *The World is Yours*. Your artistry, integrity, and cultural consciousness are appreciated.

Jahquan Hawkins – my success coach! I am forever grateful that God allowed our paths to cross. In one session, you were able to understand my character and recognize my gifts. Thank you for affirming me as an individual who is persistent *and* consistent. Both are critical for success. Thank you for all of the guidance and advice. God bless you and your family!

Anthony "Ant" Green! Man, your photography and cinematography skills are much appreciated. Thank you for being as cool as you are professional.

I want to send a special thank you to every family member who has been instrumental in my development and success throughout life. Marie (ReRe) - Thank you for allowing me to share your story with the world. Sheila, Tracy, Vanessa, PeRita, Larry, Victor, Antonio, Greg, and Uncle Herman; I love you all, and thank God for you! Many of my life lessons are the product of your guidance. Thank you for always being in my corner. To my sister-in-law, nieces, cousins, uncles, and best friends - I love you to the moon and back! To my grandparents, who are smiling down on me from heaven – I love you and miss you dearly. Thank you all for the roles you played in my life.

"You should write a book about what you love." Marc Anthony (son of Tone Merkerson), I did it! Although you are just a little one, thank you for believing in me.

Latoya NaShae Riley-Thank you for your help.

I want to extend my deepest appreciation to my social media family and friends who have supported me during this journey.

You guys are amazing! The endorsements, reviews, and comments are all appreciated.

To those who are reading *This World is Yours*, I am grateful for your support. May the Lord bless and keep you as you press on toward success.

Thank you to every person who helped in the release of this project! I am forever grateful...

# INTRODUCTION

*"Begin with the end in mind."*
-Stephen Covey

Every individual is subject to time. We all receive the same 24 hours and 365 days per year to accomplish our goals and strive toward a life of fulfillment. Take a second for self-assessment. At the end of each day/month/year, have you accomplished all that you set out to do? Ouch. That might sting a little.

Think on this: We are driven by internal and external forces. These push us toward the life of our dreams. God, family, needs, wants, money (or lack thereof), purpose, education, career advancement, lusts - you get the picture. Virtually, any and everything has the potential to play a role in how we navigate through our day-to-day existence. Those who are tenacious refuse to quit until success is achieved. When one goal is

## INTRODUCTION

reached, another is set. The pattern continues until the desired end is attained. Along the path to destiny, introspective questions are bound to arise:

*What am I seeking?*
*Are these goals worth the many sacrifices I am making?*
*Am I qualified to achieve this?*

Our vision – that which is first seen in the heart before being perceived by sight – is shaped by our answers to these and many other questions. We go for what we want. Our energy and efforts are directed toward an image that is greater than our current reality. Wherever we are when that idea or mental picture hits, our heart is our beginning and, as Covey said, "We begin with the end in mind."

Think of someone who has absolutely, positively, no desire whatsoever to impact the world around them. Hopefully, you can't. Hopelessness engulfs the person who feels as though their existence serves no purpose. Life is a gift, granted by God to each of us, for the carrying out of a unique mission. Our time on earth is not meant to be wasted, but rather, appreciated and wisely spent. We are designed for forward motion. Without progression, there is no acceleration or elevation.

"I prefer to remain stagnant," said no one ever! Truthfully, we all encounter seasons when we are less motivated than usual. Can we commit to not lingering in the mundane, or becoming content with falling behind, for extended periods? I know what it's like to be under the weight of negative emotions. Although breaking loose is difficult, we must persevere towards clarity and freedom. When I got sick and tired of being sick and tired, I pushed back against every force that tried to keep me stuck – even my own limiting mindset. I partnered my grind with ambition because 'faith without works is dead.' Giving up wasn't an option, because God created me for greater. I have no doubt that you are destined for exceedingly, abundantly, beyond what you could ask or imagine, as well.

According to Matthew chapter 28, the authority of Jesus has been granted to every believer. That's you and me! Believe that you are purposefully powerful. Run, jump, and soar to new heights! Everything that's needed is inside of you to excel in the earth. If you are unsure of how to begin, this book is the perfect start!

Consider *The World is Yours* as your go-to guide for goal exercises, which lead to guaranteed success. Within it are practical strategies proven to propel you toward achieving your objectives. Having a solid foundation is of utmost importance, so we will be sure that yours is rock-solid enough to handle the vastness and vision of your future endeavors. After all, success requires strategies. The purpose of this book is to work (yes, work, not walk) you through the process of setting goals, developing action plans, and implementing those strategies to see the manifestation of your desired result.

Is that scary *and* exciting? Probably so, but don't worry! I'll be with you every step of the way. Woven throughout the book are key points that contribute to my fortitude and professional accomplishments. These aren't things that I've made up; I live

INTRODUCTION

them daily. These principles reflect who I am and the values on which I stand. If you commit to doing the work, you will experience measurable results that produce life transformation.

Soon, you will see that "goal achiever" looks good on you! So, are you ready to level up to become all that God has called you to be? Let's begin... with the end in mind.

# THE IMPORTANCE OF PERSISTENCE

*If you want something bad enough
and you have the desire, you'll walk to another
state or country if you have to."*

-Sean "P. Diddy" Combs

**P**ersistence: Firm or obstinate continuance in a course of action, in spite of difficulty or opposition.

Mindset determines how we move from our current situation to more desirable circumstances. On the journey to achieving our goals and dreams, persistence is a must! As I reflect on Google's definition of persistence, I can't help but see it as an unwavering force of determination that refuses to stop, or change, until success is reached. Per-sis-STANCE. It is taking the stance that quitting is not an option. Personal persistence is the process of firmly placing one foot in front of the other to advance toward your vision or goal. It is the resolve to tenaciously endure until aspirations materialize. Are you as familiar with the crucial need for persistence as I am?

> *"And I tell you, ask, and it will be given to you; seek, and you will find; knock, and it will be opened to you. For everyone who asks receives, and the one who seeks finds, and to the one who knocks it will be opened."* -Luke 11:9-10 (ESV)

Persistence is the catalyst that moves us toward an expected hope and a future. *Ask.* What is it that you most strongly desire? *Seek.* How far is it from your grasp? *Knock.* Do you have the courage to believe in yourself and go for it? Just as we are to be progressive, consistent, and fervent in petitioning the Father in prayer, we should also enlist those same qualities when running this race called life. Without endurance, success becomes nothing more than a wish. Sometimes, miraculous provision occurs by faith alone; other times, we are empowered to sow good works and reap a bountiful harvest of desired outcomes. 'Faith is the substance of things hoped for' and persistence is the vehicle that gets us to our individual places of promise and achievement.

Wait a minute. All this talk of persistence and endurance might have you feeling overwhelmed. It's okay! That's exactly why we are here together. My plan is to help you set and achieve your goals. Through *The World is Yours*, my intention is to impart strategies, spiritual principles, and specific qualities necessary for successfully accomplishing your goals. You might be thinking, *Tamieka, what qualifies you to help me? What makes you such an expert?* The answer is "time." Time has confirmed that, not only am I goal-oriented and persistent, but that over and over again, my master plans produce results, according to the Master's plan.

Having well-developed strategies doesn't mean I was without struggles and stumbling blocks. Fires, storms, disappointments, and loss – you name it – I have experienced it. But, you know what? Through it all, I never doubted my ability to win. Neither do I doubt your ability to persevere through every obstacle that comes your way. If staying the course seems like a hassle, then you are on the right journey with the perfect partner. You are reading this book at the appointed time and are being instructed by a God-appointed person in the ways of persisting until the vision comes to fruition. I am not giving up on you, and you aren't going to give up on yourself. We are in this together.

We all have dreams and goals. If I'm not mistaken, that's exactly why you are here! Beyond personal aspirations, each of us has a God-given purpose to accomplish. The same holds true for divine purpose and ambitious dreams; envisioning the end result inspires us to action. Developing a strategy prepares us for forward motion. Having a clear picture in our minds motivates us to bust through boundaries, and step over stumbling blocks, by serving as a constant reminder that there is more to life than what we have already experienced. The weightier the goal, the more value we ascribe to it, and the more likely we are to persist until success is achieved.

Regardless of whether your goal is short-term or long-term, how badly you want it is the critical factor that determines if you develop, and stick to, an action plan to achieve it. Still, gifts, talents, and abilities are not enough to propel you forward! Since this notion is contrary to popular belief, allow me to repeat it once more for emphasis. *Our gifts, talents, and abilities alone will not get us to our desired goal or purpose.* Specific steps must be taken. I'll be honest with you (as I intend to be throughout this entire journey), our action steps must include developing key character traits and qualities. Persistence is mentioned first because nothing is achieved without it. Also, it just so happens to be my best quality.

Sometimes our strength can be a weakness. Even still, there are lessons to be learned. Although I have a lifetime's worth of persistence stories, there's one particular goal I would like to share with you – law school. Of course, this would be a challenge, but can you relate to desperately wanting something that's guaranteed to stretch you? Maybe that promotion requires an additional ten hours of work per week. Or perhaps, as rewarding as it is, parenthood is placing unimaginable physical, emotional, and possibly spiritual demands on you that weren't previously anticipated. Ahh, now you get it! The manifestation of anything great requires that we increase our capacity.

The thought of law school impassioned me. I just *knew* this was my true calling and the purpose for which God had created me. Whew! I am here to transparently tell you that it is possible to persist in the wrong direction. I *also* want to let you know that, as long as you are learning and growing, no target is completely missed.

So, here we go. Around the age of 31, I began the law school journey. *Thousands* of dollars were invested in the fulfillment of this goal. Kaplan Law School test preparation programs, an accelerated preparation course, and *multiple* admissions tests between 2003 and 2013; you name it, I did it for an entire decade while in pursuit of my Juris Doctorate. That might sound outlandish to you, but for me, the time, effort, and money were worth it. Within me exists an unquenchable hunger for knowledge; I love to be educated and to educate others. The funny thing is my desire was never to practice law. I know! You're thinking, *what, T. Lee?!* No, my passion was pointed in the direction of teaching on a collegiate level. I saw my calling as being lived out in the classroom rather than in the courtroom.

I purchased study guides and a copy of Black's Law Dictionary. Thoughts of graduating from law school consumed my mind. I persisted because, well, what would be the sense in quitting? After purchasing countless books and a ton of self-study hours, my LSAT scores were still quite low. They didn't even meet the minimum requirement for admission. What did I do? I persevered! This time, I hired a personal tutor to assist me with the logic portion of the exam. I received *two* conditional admissions into law school programs. The problem is I failed one of the two courses for both programs. Ugh!

*Why is this such a struggle?*
*They see me trying. Why not just let me in?*
*How much more is this going to take?*

What questions do you ask yourself when your dream seems to be so close, yet so far? By this point, I was frustrated and deeply invested financially. Think about it. In addition to courses and books, I was out of money for a laptop, study guides, a microphone headset, and travel expenses. Oh, I was getting this degree! Besides personal willpower, having others believe in me was adding fuel to the fire. I had supportive family and friends who had no doubt that I could do this. Why would they believe otherwise? I have a reputation for setting and conquering goals. No one expected this to be any different.

Embarrassment started to kick in. I began telling people that I passed the LSAT, but financial aid issues were preventing me from starting school. Hey! Don't judge. At the moment, a lie was easier to articulate than the truth. I was disappointed in myself and could not bear the thought of people thinking that I couldn't make the cut. I reasoned in my mind that a law degree was my pathway to teaching at a university.

During my ten-year pursuit, my LSAT scores ranged from 129-139; a score of 143 was needed to gain acceptance. Sigh. My score was so close and yet not close enough. Eventually, I had to be honest about my journey. *I didn't get in. Period!*

We each have a unique path assigned to our lives. I began to realize that my plan was not God's plan. Although I had invested much time, money, and effort, being in the will of God was more important. I finally laid my plans of continuing to persevere towards law school to rest.

*Who am I?*
*What has God placed within me?*
*How can I impact those around me?*

Instead of sulking about an unachieved dream, I shifted my perspective in order to gain insight regarding my identity. I am persistent. Teaching is a passion that does not have to be confined to law. I have a valuable voice to offer the world, backed by a wellspring of experience! It's okay if the one goal didn't pan out. Could it be that the true purpose of my pursuit was to reveal who I am and how my gifts should be applied? You see, a loss is only a loss when you refuse to look beneath the surface to discover the lesson.

Some would say that this experience was best kept quietly tucked in my past. I say, you deserve a look at my flaws *and* fruition. What good is it to have a know-it-all guide who can't relate to your struggles? Absolutely no good at all! Anything less than an authentic view of my full picture would be a disservice to you. I understand that not every goal comes easily. In this pursuit, all was not lost. Our messes and mistakes have built-in messages. Here is mine: My law school journey further developed me in knowledge, wisdom, patience, and determination. You have to figure out what story is hidden in your struggle.

## ORIGINAL INDIVIDUAL

*"I'm one of the few that's true."*
-Renardo Lee

I am forthcoming about my flaws, but this journey requires being honest and authentic with yourself. Being goal-oriented necessitates self-awareness. Take a second to imagine the life of your dreams. Goals are accomplished, and all is as you hoped it would be.

Your path – no matter the ups and downs – was tailor-made for you. It brought you to this manifested place of fulfillment and success. Now, think about how impossible this reality would be if you were oblivious to what gives you joy, pushes you to strive, or frustrates you to the point of complacency. What would be the result of not knowing your pain points or being able to identify what angers you?

Who we are isn't always super cut and dry. At times, we fall in-between extrovert and introvert, life of the party and wallflower, or passive and aggressive. Knowing our unique positions in these categories provide clues as to who we are as individuals, and how we work toward success. Notice that I said, "work toward success." No matter how you are wired, success is achievable. Never, under any circumstances, should you fall and stay down. Have some fight in you! Got knocked down? Okay, so get back up! A lack of awareness and tenacity hinders us from experiencing the good and hope-filled life promised in God's Word. *Wait.* Let that soak in. Living with a revelation of who you are provides the zeal needed to propel you into the life you are destined to have.

Understanding who we are in the present helps pinpoint the necessary changes that enable us to get to where we are going. We have to be real with ourselves. Which qualities should remain? Which ones need enhancing or eliminating? Acknowledging the good, and addressing the not-so-good, provides a boost of confidence that fuels us to run this race with endurance. You have a lane that only you can master. Faith, self-awareness, and personal growth work together to empower you to believe in you. You have to know that you can reach any level! So, what if it's bigger than anything you've ever accomplished before? Hey, there's a first time for everything!

We all get one life to live and one lane in which to run. Your race isn't my race; neither is mine yours. However, I believe we both have the foundational gifts, talents, and skills required to start putting one foot in front of the other. It's up to us to cultivate our God-given abilities, hone our skills, and weed out any hindrances that serve as potential distractions and stumbling blocks along the way.

We may as well address the hard stuff. Trials, persecution, misplaced desires, haters, and bad habits are a part of life. No one is exempt. As unique as your identity and your path to greatness are, so are your individual hardships. Although difficulty comes to oppose your success, be of good cheer because Jesus has overcome the world, and so will you!

In the eyes of God, you are valuable *and* victorious! I strongly encourage you to know who you are, remember why you started this journey, and remain confident in knowing you can do this! Now is the season when you resolve to trust God and live out His plan for your life. Persistence begins to dwindle when our vision becomes blurred. We trip over all that could go wrong instead of approaching life optimistically. Let's review the Parable of the Sower (Mark 4:13-20, ESV):

> "And He said to them, "Do you not understand this parable? How then will you understand all the parables? The sower sows the Word. And these are the ones by the wayside where the Word is sown. When they hear, Satan comes immediately and takes away the Word that was sown in their hearts.
>
> These, likewise, are the ones sown on stony ground who,

when they hear the Word, immediately receive it with gladness; and they have no root in themselves, and so endure only for a time. Afterward, when tribulation or persecution arises for the Word's sake, immediately they stumble.

Now, these are the ones sown among thorns; they are the ones who hear the Word, and the cares of this world, the deceitfulness of riches, and the desires for other things entering in choke the Word, and it becomes unfruitful.

But these are the ones sown on good ground, those who hear the Word, accept it, and bear fruit: some thirtyfold, some sixty, and some a hundred."

Satan comes to knock us off our square. He hates when we press forward in God! Press on anyway. Be determined to fulfill the call on your life no matter what. Stop looking around; look straight ahead. Go for the goal of being the most original, highly successful individual version of you! The Dramatics say, *"You can change, but you can't conceal what's inside of you."*[1]

It's tempting to become burdened by the passing weeks, months, and maybe even years. Naawww! Let that go. Comparison kills! This is not the time for people-pleasing and conforming to their opinions. Rather than becoming distracted by the calendar and where you feel you should be by now, trust what's in you. Know that you are a game-changer. Keep your eyes on the prize and dominate your path. When you do, success is inevitable. Setbacks happen, but that's not our focus.

You are here with me so that I can provide the motivation that leads to your continued momentum. Keep running your race! Confess that you are a winner, because you *are* a winner.

# MAKE LIGHT OUT OF YOUR VISION

*"It's pretty hard for the Lord to guide you
if you haven't made up your mind which way to go."*
-Madame C. J. Walker

Goals are the starting line for personal growth, but where do goals originate? Vision is the motivation for getting started. It is the inner picture of your determined future. Vision is seeing your hopes and dreams come true before they materialize. Have you ever experienced a time when you were knocking out one goal after another, only to find yourself struggling to remain motivated? If so, you most likely were chasing success rather than vision.

> "Now faith is the substance of things
> hoped for, the evidence of things not seen."
> -Hebrews 11:1

A vision is intangible and yet still concrete. It is attached to a purpose that is bigger than any one individual, and it's backed by faith. It has substance long before it comes to pass. Vision is powerful because it brings clarity, and once it manifests, a new level of fulfillment is experienced. When we aimlessly pursue success without purpose in mind, achievements fall flat, leaving us to search for the next "feel good" thing. Winning isn't winning when the substance of purpose isn't involved. Goals are specific targets that require strategies to be achieved. When vision is the target, goals are the pathway to meaningful success.

> *"It is one place you have not looked, and it is there, only there, that you shall find the master."* -The Last Dragon

I love this quote! *The Last Dragon* is one of my *favorite* movies. If you haven't seen it, check it out! I promise, you won't regret it. Leroy needed to envision himself as the master, or else he would never become a Kung Fu Master. He had to find his "glow" and he did. The answer was within him all along; all he had to do was correctly see his future self. You have to see your future self.

When we become unshakable and unmovable in our decision to achieve a goal, a fire ignites. Keeping that vision at the forefront of our minds serves as the fuel for persistent action.

The more precise we are regarding our wants, needs, and "non-negotiables," the clearer the vision becomes. The clearer the vision, the better we are positioned to create a sequence of short and long-term goals that ultimately lead us to the life of our dreams. Step- by-step and goal-by-goal, we ascend to the next level of greatness. True vision has value, and that value empowers your entire being – spirit, mind, and body.

Full engagement of every part of you is needed for achievement. Remain focused on the vision before you. Doing so will demand excellence in conduct and extraordinary determination in your daily walk of faith. Precise vision lights the way to a bright future.

Identity is connected to destiny, but destiny will not be reached without vision. Dream big; meditate on God's promises; persist to achieve every goal. As you persist, be sure to remain in alignment with the Lord's will. His ways are higher than our ways; His thoughts are higher than our thoughts (Isaiah 55:8-9). Unquestionably, His plan runs circles around ours, so let's be sure to go for the God-goals above all else. They are undeniably more magnificent than anything we could ever imagine.

The mere fact that you are still on this journey lets me know that you have potential and persistence. Don't give up. Don't stop now! Les Brown, one of my favorite inspirational speakers, says, "You have greatness in you!" I am confident that you have a vision that is empowering you to become greater than great. You have an inner visionary. Like, "Bruce Leroy," you have that "Master glow!"

# YOUR MIND IS A TERRIBLE THING TO WASTE

*"Your life is as good as your mindset."*
-Unknown

I have no doubt that you can achieve your wildest dreams! God endows every individual with specific gifts, talents, and abilities to execute the call He places on their lives. Maintaining a positive mindset is a part of the mandate. Doing so is a primary key to moving forward into your bright future of promise. We become what we believe about ourselves.

Henry Ford said, "Whether you think you can or you can't, you're right." That's so true! It echoes the words of Proverbs 23:7: "As a man thinks in his heart, so is he." We become defeated in our minds before anything else has a chance to knock us down. Both Henry Ford and the Lord let us know that thoughts are powerful. Honestly, we are sometimes entirely too critical of ourselves; we become our own worst enemy and our thoughts become crippling weights that prevent us from taking action. Instead, let's focus on empowering truths.

As we tend to go in the direction of our cravings, vision is important! It is the driving force that gets us to where we are going. When there is a clear picture in our hearts, hunger for the vision is produced. This isn't an overly spiritual concept. Take a few seconds to think about your favorite food. You have the mental picture? Perfect. How does it smell? Is it salty, sweet, or savory? I bet your mouth is watering now! Ha! When I get hungry for chicken wings or pizza, the craving refuses to leave until it is satisfied. Envisioning your future produces a form of hunger; it keeps the goal on your mind and in your heart until it is achieved.

> "A hope deferred makes the heart sick, but when the desire comes, it is a tree of life."
> -Proverbs 13:12 (ESV)

Maintain sight of the hope that is in your heart. God planted it there to produce a vision, and vision that is partnered with persistence will surely come to pass. The enemy comes with distractions and derailments to bully us out of our promises. Naturally and spiritually, strategic assaults are targeted in our direction to get us off track. Stand firm. *Press on.*

I know I'm on the winning side, and so are you! If you aren't entirely convinced, keep reading. Belief is about to rise up in you!

Begin each day with intentionality to preserve your thought life. Give more consideration to the thoughts you're entertaining. According to the *Financial Post*, the human mind can produce up to 50,000 thoughts per day. Of those half a million thoughts, as much as 80% of them are negative.[1] Whew! With so much negativity swirling around in our heads, being passive won't cut it. Mind management needs to begin in the morning and continue to last throughout the day.

Okay. Now you're saying, "But T. Lee, my mind gets hit daily!" Trust me . . . I get it. Let's consider some patterns. Telemarketers and debt collectors start calling first thing in the morning. We often scroll through social media news feeds while still in bed. Before our feet touch the floor, we begin ingesting negativity, mass hysteria, faithless opinions, and shame. Thousands of thoughts are initiated that work against our hope for the future. This is why it is so crucial that we filter our thoughts and choose – yes, choose – to think on good things. Thinking differently is a choice. You have the power to take authority over your thoughts.

> "Finally, brothers, whatever is true, whatever is honorable, whatever is just, whatever is pure, whatever is lovely, whatever is commendable, if there is any excellence, if there is anything worthy of praise, think about these things." -Philippians 4:8 (ESV)

Thinking on all that is good sounds great, but how? Shifting our thought life requires mind renewal. There are a number of ways to do it, but I'll share what works for me. I begin every single day with prayer, praise, reading Scripture, or listening to some old school music that motivates me.

"And be not conformed to this world: but be ye transformed by the renewing of your mind, that ye may prove what is that good, and acceptable, and perfect, will of God."
-Romans 12:2

Mind renewal is the beginning of faith-based optimism. In addition to spending time with God and in His Word, I listen to and watch programs that keep me calm, positive, and focused. For the last three to four years, I've been devouring messages by Les Brown, Tony Robbins, and Eric "ET" Thomas. These guys boost my mental state. My outlook began to change over time. Because my mind was being conditioned to think positively, I began to see positively. Mentality and vision go hand-in-hand. Find what works for you – comedy, uplifting songs, anything that gets your thoughts going in the right direction will do. We have to feed our faith instead of fueling our doubts.

Expect better . . . experience better.

I'll be honest with you. Suspicion was once my stumbling block. I trusted no one. Oh yeah, I was saved and sitting under excellent teaching. I even read *Battlefield of the Mind* by Joyce Meyer *twice*. No results. I was still thinking, speaking, and acting crazy.

Here's the problem: Distrust wasn't helping me; it was hurting me. Multiple relationships were being negatively affected, and I was the common denominator. Something had to change... and that something was me. This mindset of suspicion rooted in fear was blocking my happiness. It was stunting my growth. It had to go! I started thinking about my thoughts, taking every negative one captive to God's truth. The weight lifted; my heart was lighter. My mind was clearer. Was it an overnight transformation? No, but I did change. Discipline has a way of reconstructing the details of our everyday lives. We can do whatever we are disciplined to set our minds to, including improving our thought patterns.

When reality keeps failing to match our efforts, it's time to evaluate our thoughts. No, that doesn't mean beat ourselves up for not having it all together. That does nothing but produce more stress, anxiety, and worry. What I am saying is that we must take inventory of our thought life and actively work towards cleaning it up. I submit to you that we have mind control. Rather than moping over lack and disappointment, we can shift our mindset toward fruitful and flourishing thoughts. We win at life when we conquer our thoughts. Whatever your aspirations may be, a believing mindset is required to achieve success.

Your purpose is essential. It was gifted to you by God; your presence is needed in this generation. That dream that keeps you up at night? It's not an accident. It is an intentional vision bestowed upon you by the Father. The future you envision is far more than a lingering thought. It is a divine craving that requires persistence, and the right mindset to come to fruition. Believe me when I tell you that it is attainable.

    You can do it! Believe in yourself. Focus on progressing day-by-day. Remain optimistic. Think deeply, dream big, and know that you have a destiny that is unlimited. Confess over yourself, "My vision is blessed and prosperous!"

    Believe that you can accomplish the impossible.

# MORE DISCIPLINE, MUCH CLOSER

*"We must all suffer one of two things:
the pain of discipline or the pain of regret."*
-Jim Rohn

Success is neither easy nor random. It will never simply fall into our laps without intentional effort on our part. As much as we would like to avoid it, work is required. The process of goal achievement demands focus and discipline.

Wait! Before you start thinking of discipline as punishment or forced correction, consider it as an opportunity to create positive results. Rather than an authority figure barking orders, the discipline of our focus is the product of self-control and determination. Take a second to ask yourself this question: *Am I disciplined?* If you are, great! That's half of the battle. If not, know that you can become such an individual.

Discipline is a code of behavior, and behavior can be modified and developed with effort. We are referring to positive self-restraint that propels individuals forward while developing life skills and increasing personal growth.

I know, from personal experience, how easy it is to get off course and lose focus. When I began college at Wayne State University, I was disciplined. Earning my degree was motivation for maintaining the tunnel vision needed to achieve my educational goals. Then, things took a turn during my sophomore year; zeal was lost as my interest shifted. My attention span was at an all-time low. Instead, hanging out and smoking marijuana increased. My grades dropped. I worked so hard to get to this point, but now, my actions were putting my education and financial aid in jeopardy.

One day, the lightbulb just clicked. I had to take responsibility for my actions. Never let anyone tell you it's not okay to talk to yourself. Sometimes you have to encourage yourself. If you're like me, at other times you have to lecture yourself. *You came here to earn that bachelor's degree, and you're going to get it!* From that moment forward, I began aligning my actions with my aspirations. Distance was placed between my "kick it crew" and me. Did I enjoy hanging out? Absolutely! However, my future was more important than partying. Distractions could not be given more attention than my dreams.

The good news is that I did graduate, although it took five years instead of four. That's okay. The important thing is that I accomplished the very goal I set out to achieve. Self-inflicted setbacks and all, I regained focus, became disciplined, and earned my degree! Now, the bad news is that, while I did eventually stop smoking weed, it didn't happen immediately. It is much easier to avoid a bad habit than to break one. The Bible is clear on the importance of discipline:

> "Whoever is slack in his work
> is a brother to him who destroys."
> -Proverbs 18:9 (ESV)

> "Love not sleep, lest you come to poverty;
> open your eyes, and you will have plenty of bread."
> -Proverbs 20:13

You are full of potential; your future is full of promise. Please do not be the cause of your own destruction. Work hard and progress. Now, you may wonder what's needed to become a disciplined person. Let me emphasize the fact that discipline doesn't come easily for everyone. For some, it's a piece of cake; it is a struggle for others. There are levels to this. Even if you work full or part-time, I want to encourage you by letting you know that your goals do not have to be placed on the backburner; list your priorities and create a plan of action for taking care of them. Create space in your daily routine to work towards your endeavor. Times flies, so make the most of it by remaining disciplined.

Here's a helpful hint: If you aren't making technology work

for you, it might be working against you. So much is at our fingertips. Getting sucked into random text message conversations and social media scrolling and swiping jeopardizes the fulfillment of our goals. The more time we waste on meaningless pastimes, the less time we have to devote to purpose. I am merely suggesting that you be mindful of how your time is delegated. Maybe that post can wait until later. Surely, your friends will understand if you knock out a few items on your to-do list before returning their calls. Your favorite show comes on tonight! Maybe consider watching it On Demand or stream it at a later date.

Keeping *first things first* makes discipline doable. Delayed gratification is no less gratifying. In all honesty, it might be a little sweeter. You get to enjoy the things you love, along with the satisfaction of knowing what you have accomplished.

There are times when I silence my phone and avoid listening to music or watching television. Thoughts might cross my mind like, "I can work on this tomorrow," or "Watch *Beat Street* or *Krush Groove*." I might be tempted to call someone or go visit. Instead, I choose to embrace positive isolation as a means of helping me focus on the task at hand. Instead of going out to eat and running the risk of having my time stolen by instant pleasures, I cook or order delivery. This is a simple, yet effective strategy that gets the job done. My life doesn't revolve around work, but when it's time to get down to business, these are the measures I take.

As a matter of fact, I had to apply strict discipline to write these words. Oh yeah! My wandering mind wanted to watch an old school movie or visit family. But, I just said, "Nope, I'm going to finish writing this book."

If you think distractions won't come your way, you are mistaken. My sincere prayer is that you refuse to be stopped in your pursuit of purposeful success. Remember, persistence causes discipline to reign over an idle mind and lazy hands. Place a demand on your life (as in on yourself) to be organized, and then stick to the plan.

Do not be moved by your emotions! You may not feel like working out, but if becoming an award-winning bodybuilder is the goal, hitting the gym is a must. Please be aware of the relationship drama that comes to knock you off course. I know what it's like to be so upset by a failed relationship that goals get forgotten. This is why it is so crucial to know who you are and what you want out of life. Your commitments are to you and for you, not the person in your past who has no place in your future. If negative emotions currently have you stuck, snap out of it! Evaluate your thoughts. Choose to think about good things like love, joy, peace, and prosperity. Be resilient, and keep moving forward!

Consider the areas in your life where more focus and self-restraint are needed. Try to make the necessary adjustments. Goals require thorough attention and strategic planning, so comb through every detail. Discipline creates a healthy work ethic that will lead to the development of positive habits. When your mindset and actions align, it's like comedian J. Anthony Brown says, "Watch out there now!" You're ready for success!

Right thinking and intentional behaviors position you for

destiny. Your desired result will be the reward of your disciplined life. So, I encourage you to deliberately move toward your goals, dreams, and calling. You can do it! By faith, I believe that you have the necessary will power to be disciplined in the execution of your action plan. No matter the obstacles or defeating thoughts, go for your goals. Trust that discipline will create the stability needed to continue pressing forward.

As Jim Rohn states, "Discipline is the bridge between goals and accomplishments." Whatever it will take for you to become more disciplined, just know that you can move closer to achieving your goals and live out your dreams.

# ARE YOU CONSISTENT ENOUGH?

*"Dedication, hard work, and routine build character."*
-Nasir "Nas" Jones

Often, success is attributed to a number of factors: intelligence, creativity, appearance, connections, and even willingness to persist. It can be assumed that those who have any of these going for them will experience higher levels of achievement. Research reveals that it is indeed true, and in certain fields, attractiveness and other physical attributes play a significant role. Thankfully, looks do not define your ability or capacity to reach your goals, so please don't get sidetracked.

The mastery of a skill, learning a new technique, and lifestyle changes all require consistent diligence. Consistency is a major key to accomplishing anything; it is a highly important character trait needed to reach your goals.

*The World is Yours* is not designed to make you an overnight success or give you step-by-step instructions for a get-rich-quick scheme. The main focus is to instill necessary qualities that will develop your archetype for goal achievement. It is my aim to teach you the qualities that others love to duplicate. Admiration isn't always about money. Sometimes, others strive to mimic our patterns and behavior because of the tenacity we exude, the confidence with which we carry ourselves, or the stellar work ethic we possess. Maybe it's our wisdom, or knowledge, that catches their attention. People look up to others for various reasons.

For example, I think everyone admires the iconic boxer, Muhammad Ali. Although he was undefeated and globally recognized, it was somewhat his reputation for being a trash talker that captured everyone's attention. Ali was as consistent as he was confident, which allowed him to overcome any opponent who stepped into the ring with him. His consistent confidence made him unforgettable, and his daughter, Laila Ali, has mastered her father's qualities. She leaned into the skills he taught and voila! She is a phenomenal, trash-talking boxer full of confidence, just like her father. Their words inspire me to be consistent in speaking victory into reality, and I want you to get to this point as well.

Consistency has many definitions, but I want to focus on a particular one from Dictionary.com: *steadfast adherence to the same principles, course, form, etc.* I am using this version because of the word *steadfast*. Steadfastness requires having loyalty and commitment to a thing; it is having faith and dedication. Steadfastness is giving your all to a goal - doing it with all of your heart and soul until completion. It is a key ingredient often left out by many people. Allow me to reiterate that, in order to be successful, consistency is commitment, and commitment is dedication. Being consistent is a long-term way of being. Even if you're working towards a short-term goal, remain consistent for the required period and see how sweet the results will be.

Now, you know I have to show what the Word of God says about consistency! Operating with consistency is an admirable trait that produces good fruit when the goal is good. It is possible to be consistent in the wrong thing and end up with bad fruit. Hebrews 13:7 states, "Remember your leaders, those who spoke to you the Word of God. Consider the outcome of their way of life, and imitate their faith" (ESV). Those who accept Jesus as Lord and Savior dedicate their lives to following His ways. They serve with their whole hearts and consistently live out the Word of Truth. They are prudent and faithful. These are people who consistently pursue their goal of pleasing God.

If your heart is to achieve a particular goal, set your faith to it, and remain diligent. You never know whose inspiration you'll become! Let your conduct be worthy of imitation. Shine bright, be consistent, and apply faithfulness to the completion of your plan. This is especially important if you have children or youth who look up to you.

Having follow-through says a lot about your character. Consistent pursuit of your objectives shows that you are responsible, dedicated, and reliable. Professional athletes put in countless hours of practice to be the best. Highly sought-after beauticians are committed to being on time for their appointments and serving their clients in excellence. Entrepreneurship requires daily focus and dedication to maintain productivity and success. Likewise, an employer hires those who are skilled in their trade and consistent in their work ethic. Words and actions should not contradict one another. When the two don't align, don't beat yourself up. It happens. Just remember that, once you decide to complete a goal, live it out. There is nothing you can't do!

Life happens. Situations will arise that cause a deviation of plans. Do you remember the 'Parable of the Sower' that we discussed in a previous chapter? The key is to be an overcomer, even when things shift unexpectedly. That is how you obtain the reward. When God's Word is heard and applied, it takes root and provides a foundation on which we can stand. The Word that is honored, and consistently applied, will bear fruit. If you remain diligent along the path to success, you will prosper. Allow consistency to triumph over the distractions, disappointments, and people who attempt to prevent you from moving forward.

Losing focus is a temptation from time to time. We sometimes lose sight of our intended goal. Although distractions and disappointments are sure to come, those who remain consistent have decided to stay on track, no matter what issues may arise along the way. It's inevitable that you will get knocked down, make a mistake, or even fail. When that happens, consistency will prompt you to create a new strategy; press toward the desired outcome.

I have made simple mistakes and experienced failure. However, I chose not to consistently dwell in a place of hurt, pain, loss, or lack of wisdom in the moment. I picked myself back up with a renewed mind and a genuine smile. I move forward with a clear heart and a clean spirit. It is imperative that we acknowledge our mistakes and learn from our failures. When we make a conscious effort to do so, winning will be the result rather than losing. In reality, failures and mistakes aren't as bad as we often make them out to be. They are learning opportunities that equip us to do better the next time. Go hard every step of the way to finish strong.

I will forewarn you though, you will shed some tears. I've cried like a baby over things like not accomplishing a goal, being passed over for a job, not being paid my worth, and failed relationships. Even though we exercise consistency, some things simply are not meant to be. Don't lose hope . . . persist. If you need to cry, let it all out. Choose resilience rather than a "woe is me" mentality. Step out of misery and into thankfulness. Yes, thank God in advance for the prize that awaits you!

You will win because *the world is yours*.

## YOU MUST LEARN

*"Every addition to true knowledge
is an addition to human power."*
- Horace Mann

Every goal must be obtained by getting knowledge, understanding, wisdom, and insight. Too often, we miss the fine print, which includes the main details. This is because we don't take the time to read and research. We may forget to weigh the outcomes of the goals we are seeking, whether good or bad. In all things, we must try to obtain a clear understanding. Proverbs 4:7 says, "Wisdom is the principal thing; therefore, get wisdom; and with all thy getting, get understanding."

You gain knowledge, understanding, and wisdom by asking questions. You ask, 'Who? What? When? Where? Why? And how?' Gaining knowledge is a process. This is why you have to attend school from the day you're born until you decide when you will graduate. Even then, our life's experiences are a sum total of what we have learned and will learn. However, knowledge is not only gained by asking questions, it's also about faith, intuition, and following your spirit guide. Sometimes we are even led by our emotions, in which we obtain knowledge from our emotions; we learn what to do and what not to do.

Knowledge can be acquired in a variety of ways, such as by:

- Studying the history of the goal that you're after.
- Watching a person's body language.
- Sitting in on an educational conference.
- Going to an entrepreneur seminar.
- Participating in webinars or online learning venues
- Reading a book every thirty to sixty days.
- Obtaining common sense... and using it.

Knowledge can be attained from any resource and all sources. It's all about becoming skillful in what you want to master. You may already have knowledge, but it's about your willingness to elevate to a higher level of aptitude.

In this world, we have so many choices, and one thing I know as a necessity is for us to learn as much as we can. The purpose is to gain intricate, unwavering knowledge so that, whatever you are called to do, you can master it and do it effectively and efficiently.

Gaining an educational degree gives and takes acquired knowledge, starting a business requires knowledge of that particular industry, and if you want to have and maintain a successful relationship, it also requires knowledge of the other person. A solid foundation must be created in everything. Otherwise, failure, an unwanted fall below your level or even destruction, is almost certain to happen. Knowledge is infinite. Every human being is always on a quest for intellectual growth and stimulation. I know of many times when I've messed up or made a wrong turn because I didn't ask the right questions, didn't take my time to do my research, didn't count the cost, or I just ignored all of the red flags. There were times when I moved entirely too fast, or I didn't move quickly enough and missed an opportunity. You may think the things I've mentioned have absolutely nothing to do with getting knowledge and wisdom, but they do. Gaining knowledge basically provides you with the support you need to make better decisions.

Most of us don't want to take the time out of our busy schedules and read. Do you remember the saying, "reading is fundamental"? It is! With reading, you not only acquire knowledge, but insight. You have to work, in addition to reading up on a thing. Acquiring knowledge keeps you informed, it keeps your brain healthy and active, and you gain understanding of many concepts. Do you know how much more creative and innovative you can become just by knowing more than you did yesterday? Your capacity to store knowledge is limitless, just like your future. But, if you want to limit yourself, you would cause yourself and those who look up to you a big disservice.

There will be times when people ask you questions, seeking your expertise. Give them the truth. Be confident and wise in answering their questions. When you can answer without hesitation, and you know that your answer is factual and precise, then you not only have knowledge, insight, and understanding, you also have wisdom. Now, consider yourself an O.G.

It's enlightening to see anyone with a fundamental form of truth. It's exciting to have a new way of viewing things, having a keener vision on subjects relevant to your personal growth in this world. It's refreshing when you have the ability to assist others with uncommon observations that give new positive perspectives and helps solve a problem. And, it's inspiring when you're able to connect with someone by making a clear and concise statement and sharing precise strategies by which somebody can aim towards and hit the target.

You're already this person. Don't underestimate yourself. Your dreams, goals, desires, purpose, calling, and assignment on this earth is inevitable when you're the best of your best. When you're the greatest you that you can be. When your knowledge is reliable, and your findings are documented, you're thriving. Now you know stuff!

Learn all you can and have fun in learning. When you seek and gain knowledge, new avenues are created, and your awareness level heightens; you become more of an asset. Remember, you are valuable. When you're getting knowledge and awareness of your goals, you have covered all of the basics, and you believe that you're ready to take that step, be sure to have a clear understanding – not only of the goal itself – but also of why this goal is important to you. Have an understanding of how you're going to apply this goal to your life, how application of your goal will help others. Remember, you don't put in your sweat and tears to be mediocre. You don't research for information only to be somewhat familiar with it. No! If you want a clear understanding of anything and if you're going to be above average when you're doing what you love to do, then that's when you know that you have intimate knowledge of it; now it's personal to you. You have acquired emotional intelligence, and now you see the depth of the subject.

Don't pretend! If you don't understand something, then you don't understand. It's detrimental to grasp the knowledge you have otherwise; it will be a big blur to you, and then you will be disinterested. So, before you become that police officer, or lawyer, or that engineer, or parent, or before you become that conglomerate, or before you launch that ten-million-dollar business venture, make sure you understand completely. Never say, 'Oh, I know enough,' because, more than likely, you don't. Never settle. Constantly improve yourself.

Going after any goal requires a person to get facts, get practical knowledge, which is a basic understanding, to observe and analyze or to just get directly involved. Going after any goal will require a person to gain experience. There is a saying, "Experience is a good teacher." Actually, it is not only a good teacher; it is the best. Life is an experience, and part of life is for humanity to be exposed to the fullness of all that it has to offer.

Of course, life is going to take us through some ups and downs, but, for the most part, life is not to be taken for granted. Life must be used in a way that we are fulfilled and not unfulfilled, getting meaningful experience so that we may live with growth and prosperity and not live with the regret of our life's decisions. Think of it this way . . . the way we perceive things is more often than not shaped by our life's experiences. Our life's history is cultivated based on our past and present life's experiences. This is why it is vital to try to have the best experiences possible. Our experiences sometimes push us toward our future goals, dreams, and aspirations.

At times, this becomes the primary reason for why we choose a goal, so that we can change a thing in a specific area of interest. Experience is a bit much. Yeah, everybody will have bad experiences, but so what! I'll tell you that it should be the good experiences that supersede anything. But it's with the bad experiences that we learn how to grow. Hey, you just have to learn to appreciate both.

Gaining experience is extremely personal, because we then have the opportunity to give the experience meaning and then decide to proceed or not. To reach a goal, you have to go out and live that dream. You have to just do it! You have to go and get hands-on experience. Goals are not easy to reach, and if it's easily attainable, then it's probably not your passion or God-given purpose. *Why not?* Because typically, you're going to get much-needed information, accumulating sweat and tears over time, while trying to win at that thing. So, before you dive out in the waters, be sure that you're sure and that you're ready to make that jump.

This is your experience! Your today may not be similar to your yesterday; however, it will give you a belief on how to maneuver through your life's journey and goals of tomorrow.

All that you hear will not be a fact, all that you see will not always be all there is to something. Even in the event of exploring something, there will always be a higher level. There will always be a belief, there will always be a conclusion, and there will always be biases of something. But, always keep your vision plain and in front of your eyes of that which you're going after and allow God to be your guide. No matter the changes, no matter the shaking of information that comes to distract you, no matter the inconsistencies that attempt to break your belief system, and no matter what others may try to teach you to get you to follow a particular path, always, and I mean always, trust that God's knowledge is greater.

Believe in the knowledge that you have received. But, never think you know everything, because we don't. Always be open to learning more, accepting constructive criticism and godly advice. Draw from all of the knowledge that you get from everyone. Don't let your God-given gifts be "wasted talent."[1] Research! Empower yourself. Prepare! Learn! Apply the knowledge and be patient! There is a well-known quote by an unknown voice that says, "If you are not willing to learn, no one can help you. If you are determined to learn, no one can stop you."

## UNSWERVING DETERMINATION

*"Stop looking for your purpose... Be it."*
- Dr. Wayne Dyer

Are you determined enough to reach your goals? Sometimes, you may think you are living a life that's below what you are really capable of, or you may feel you have reached your destiny. There are times when these thoughts come to mind. If there was a time in my life where these thoughts have come to my mind, then, this is when I decided that it was to re-evaluate my current position in life and prepare for the next level. It could be possible that you may have these thoughts because it's time for you to prepare for the next level.

When you're a determined person that means you have a key

quality that is sought after by employers, potential mates, and school and sports recruiters, and for many other career positions and roles. While others search for determination in someone, likewise, we should seek to be that determined individual and gain possession of that trait, if this is a quality you know you lack.

Determination is a forceful drive within. Determination is knowing and having a strong inclination that you are going to reach your highest potential, accomplish your goals, and make a decision that you will never allow anything or anyone to stop you. Some of us were determined as kids to manifest our childhood dreams into reality. Some of us did exactly as we believed, while others were destined to follow another path. There is a dream that lives inside of us that should be birthed; we should be determined enough to bring about life to that goal.

Think of someone who set a goal to start working out. The goal is set; they're determined to make this a lifestyle. A decision is made to take a day off from working out. Next thing you know, three days have passed, then a week, and the idea of consistently working out is no longer an action you're considering taking. Around day twenty-one, you no longer have the ambition to work out, your determination has faded away, and your goal has fallen by the wayside. You are a determined person; use the strength that God has given you! Work your talents and abilities to the fullest.

Never lose the tenacity and the determination to complete your desired goal. Never let what would have turned out as a completed project end up being a failed endeavor. Be determined today, *and every day,* to live a good and productive life. Be determined today to give everything you do, all you've got.

When I use to watch my favorite football team, the Seattle Seahawks, and moving to this present day, I understand why they are considered one of the best teams in the National Football League (NFL). I understand why opposing teams use so much force against the Seahawks; it's because the opposition wants to defend their team, conquer, and gain victory over the Seahawks. It's difficult to overcome such a great team.

The thing that attracted me to the Seattle Seahawks was Richard Sherman – who is now with the San Francisco 49ers. During the 2012-2013 Football season, Richard would talk so much mess, and I was like, "Who is the guy?" But, come to find out, he was able to back up his trash talking. He was not only a hard playing cornerback, but was educated as well. Then, as I watched the Seahawks play, I was fascinated and moved by their skill: their teamwork, their winning mentality, their determination, and their will to win. This is why they consistently make it to the playoffs, even if it has been a minute since they've won the Super Bowl. Ha!

You should have the qualities of a winning team with respect to what you plan on doing with your life. You should be ready to defend, conquer, and win with your goals and you should be ready to gain and master the skills you need, have that winning mentality, and be determined to succeed – attaining victory by any means necessary. Your life will throw you some curveballs, but by no means is your life a game. What you want to be in your life will take hard work on your part, but you have to persevere and be intentional about what you want to achieve that goal. *Get the job done!* (as Big Daddy Kane said).

If you have been tempted to give up, I want you to take that same energy you're using to think negatively to reverse the thoughts and think life, think living, and think big. Rethink that decision to forfeit your future, because it's possible that you are not as determined as you should be, having lost sight of why you wanted to achieve that goal in the first place.

If you have children, let your children be your motivation. Let the thought of fulfilling your God-given purpose in life be your motivation. Most of us know what we should be doing in life, but some of us have no determination because we never know what our life's purpose and mission is. Some of us are just living leisurely, wasting this precious life that matters so much. Stop this! If you are determined enough to visualize achieving your goal, then it's a great chance that you can bring it to pass.

When you become that determined person, and when you become firm in your decision to complete a goal, there are rewards and benefits that happen as a result of your decision. The most important one is, "You did it." You now have a finished project that was worth the hard work and effort.

Now, after the goal is accomplished, when you think about it, you have made God happy, you may have increased production at a job, and you may have built up happiness and joy in your heart from a task that was well done.

I read this article titled, "A staggering ninety-two percent of people that set New Year's goals never actually achieve them.

Here's How the Other eight Percent Do," by Marcel Schwantes.[1] Now, if you think about it, this title only refers to a New Year's goal and is not really referring to a specific life goal, even though fulfilling a New Year's resolution could convert to a life goal.

Put your heart into your work! Determination is called 'willpower.' To me, willpower means making a choice to grind, to sweat, to work extra hard, regardless of what comes your way. It means staying on track in order to finish your course. Inclusive with determination is knowing who you are, persistence, discipline, consistency, getting rid of that "I can't" mentality, and adopting a renewed and positive goal-oriented mindset. Maintain your confidence! Your goals are always worth grabbing. We live in this big ol' world that's full of great opportunities.

Whatever industry you're in, someone is always affected by your work. It doesn't matter if you're working in the automobile industry, coal mining industry, or oil industry, or even if you're into trading investments, stocks, or bonds. Be the difference! The determination you should have will not allow you to be an average Joe Blow. When you're determined to accomplish your goals, and you begin to slip, remember what encouraged you to pursue that goal in the first place. Your mission is valuable! Don't make your life complicated and challenging. Overcome!

# IRON SHARPENS IRON

*"When you're in this culture in our society, you can do some phenomenal things individually. But they'll never reach their full potential, unless you do them collectively, and you have to figure out how to do that."*
-Kobe Bryant

I n the process of having all of these qualities that I've mentioned thus far, I've added a lot of emphasis on the importance of being a persistent person. In the process of being a persistent person, and while reaching goals, it took me many years to understand the importance of connecting with like-minded people. Yes, it's called "networking." I was deterred from networking earlier in life because my environmental associations were people who mainly indulged in an alternative lifestyle and some with little-to-no education.

I wasn't raised in a neighborhood with predominantly white-collar workers or businessmen and women, those of a higher socioeconomic status. . . if you will. This could be considered as having an upbringing that is underprivileged. Coming from a disadvantaged environment, it is possible that the surroundings and neighborhoods will be that of low-income families, poor parenting, and family relations. Having an upbringing in these types of settings can include factors that negatively influence the trajectory of a child's life.

So, in the interim, other family members and myself were taught that anyone who was from similar stomping grounds and experienced the same type of conditions were considered to be people who were "real," and all others were considered "fake people." Fake people were considered those who were from more affluent backgrounds and neighborhoods, more of a stable family environment, or those who were more on the straight and narrow path of life. Why is this information important? It is important to know because being brought up in this type of social atmosphere and taught not to trust, or socialize with others based on specific qualifications, scars a child and shelters them from having successful relationships.

Philippians 2:3-4 says, "Do nothing from rivalry or conceit, but in humility count others more significant than yourselves. Let each of you look not only to his own interests, but also to the interests of others" (ESV) To me, this Scripture says to rid ourselves of pride and to have love and care for others.

While I was in college, I remembered my favorite college instructor, who I still look up to at this present day. He was the reason I chose Sociology as my major in college. One day, he said to the class that networking basically means kissing up to others, but he used more explicit language. He said that networking means going around people, exchanging business cards, and everyone acting as if they're important. His perception of networking partly deterred me from socializing with like-minded individuals and attending social gatherings with people who could help make a difference in my life. This wasn't good advice; therefore, I don't suggest that you adhere to it unless it's to keep you from intermingling with the wrong crowd of people – those who will damage your life, and not add value to you or your goals.

College life involved a more diverse environment, contrary to the environment I was acclimated to. I was mentally conditioned that socializing with people not like me was a "failed relationship." But . . . yes, there is a "but" . . . now I see that this was a wrong belief system, it was seriously flawed, and it was an improper mindset to have. This was totally unfair to me, and to not fully give people a chance was unfair; this is partially what is considered "prejudging folk." There is a quote by Meg Jay that says, "It's the people we hardly know, and not our closest friends who will improve our lives most dramatically."[1]

More often than not, we tend to flock with, cooperate with, have friendships with, and agree with a particular crowd of people, not really giving others a chance. Everyone should surround themselves with people who are more compatible with the future goals that they envision for their life, and with people who at least exemplify greatness in them. This life is not just about you either, so we should surround ourselves with people we can help reach a higher level and who we can instill a greater level of inspiration and reciprocity in the relationship. It's best to connect with individuals who will not tear you down mentally, but feed positive, insightful words and deeds in our lives. It makes a difference when our circles of friends or associates are those who are possibly smarter than ourselves, and who encourage us to reach our goals and full potential. Yes, we are all different, but networking and befriending a better company of people can help us stay on the right track. Always be careful and mindful.

It's okay if you still have a friend or two from your past. Most of us do maintain childhood, high school, and college friends that become lifetime friends. However, if these friends are living loosely and never changed their habits or their lifestyle, are critical of you and your dreams, aspirations, and success, and no matter how much you encourage or help them, they will not change. Let them go! I love quotes, and I heard a quote as I was typing this portion of the book, which said, "Elevation requires separation." Sometimes it's hard to do, but you have to leave the bad seeds behind.

Let unproductive friendships go unless your love for that person is great. It happens. I had several relationships like this, and I had to, over time, change the person I was; I had to change the company I kept, and I was willing to let go. Be prepared to let go of those so-called acquaintances with no vision and are hindering your success.

When networking with others, remember that you network to move forward in your goals, not to be stagnating in life. Growth in life partly involves someone who will coach, mentor, and guide you to your successful destiny. We should always maintain a positive approach, a positive outlook, a positive mindset, and, as always, sustain a positive personality when dealing with anyone. Believe in the saying that "Our attitude determines our altitude." What a true statement that is.

There are instances where you may not connect with other individuals. It may be due to conflicting personalities; some may be intimidated by you for various reasons . . . different upbringings, lifestyles, competition, or just pure jealousy or misunderstanding of who you are or who they are. Sometimes our spirits just do not resonate with someone, and it's okay if this happens; it's a part of life and nothing to be ashamed of.

Many other reasons exist, but whatever the case may be, there should not be anyone or anything that should stop you from acquiring your goal. Honestly, God is all you need, but we were not made up to do life alone. You will come to realize that people will be people. We all have to deal with others and their personality, and they have to deal with ours as well.

Our oath and goal should be to weed out the devils, the naysayers, the gossipers, the backbiters, the less inspired, and those who do not want you to prosper. These are the people who you should not want to network with. No one wants to fail in life and certainly not in relationships. Sometimes, it's inevitable, and we must leave others behind, but try not to burn a bridge. Everything in this book suggests success, including who we come into contact with.

Be genuine! Relationships should be authentic and unconditional. Whatever type of relationship you form, just be sure it's not of ill intentions, malice, and usury. Everyone should be able to bring something to the table. Don't be in a one-sided relationship and let not the "one-sided" person be you. If you have little to offer, then offer that little from your heart. Networking may or may not blossom into friendship, and that's okay. Still, whatever it shapes into, make sure you let your intentions be overt.

While networking, it is apparent that information should be exchanged; advice is given, and referrals are possibly offered or provided, and in the process of being a resource, this is where a mutual relationship is being developed.

Again, if it is not a mutually beneficial relationship, it can fail. Don't expect it to go any further because, as you can see, it's not mutual. Don't force it! Don't force your love, don't push your information and your friendship upon anyone. . . and, if you don't want what they have, don't play a game and stick around; don't mislead anyone. Networking for success is not an obligation, but it is an incentive, an excellent benefit. Trust me! Networking is a collaborating activity.

> "Two are better than one: because they have a good
> reward for their labour. For if they fall, the one will lift

up his fellow; but woe to him that is alone when he falleth: for he hath not another to help him up."

-Ecclesiastes 4:9-10

If you decide to be in groups or network with others, don't make it a habit, or fall into the idea that you have to seek approval from others in order to determine what's best for your life. You must be confident in who you are and the calling that God has placed on your life.

I would say that everyone needs encouragement. You will not experience your true greatness if you're hanging around negative, mean, discouraging, disrespectful, spiteful, and bitter people. Oh, there are more kinds out there that will try to keep you under, but that's just to name a few. Networking interaction should produce successful results in your life because the right influences can be your guide.

One last point, it has been my decision to always be around people who love me, those who genuinely care about my happiness, whether it's a personal or a business relationship. It is important to be near those who accept you, despite your flaws, shortcomings, and with whom you can be nothing and nobody but yourself. This is how we bring value to someone else's life.

Once, I asked my friend, "Do you have a vision board?" The reply was, "No, just a board of visionaries." Wow! So, network as you see fit. But, remember, the idea is to make the relationship one of quality. . . for you and them.

## CHALLENGING YOU

*"Be thankful to those who refuse to help you,
for they force you to summon upon your warrior within."*
- Unknown

How far you go in accomplishing any goals that you have set for yourself is somewhat dependent upon how you are able to stand firm on your decision to grow. It's also dependent upon your decision to overcome any obstacles, distractions, and disappointments that you are faced with.

One thing I have learned is that you can achieve all of your goals if you constantly challenge yourself. There are times when goal-setters set vague, unattainable, and unrealistic goals, which leave the individual without clarity, and their objectives cannot be quantified.

Generally speaking, this error causes procrastination and can push the person to throw their hands up and say, "To heck with this," and then that person gives up. I mean, this happens, even to the best of us. I am telling you this from personal experience because I have been there. Now that I look back on my life, it was a huge mistake not to have precision on the goal I was seeking to achieve.

When I think back on my life now and look in retrospect, I can honestly say, I may not be where I want to be, but I do know for certain that I've worked hard in my life. I've always been on fire to accomplish the goal that I believed was for me at that specific time in my life. I do know that I have been successful; I know that I have made a difference to someone's life, including my own. I can admit that I have failed and have learned from my failures, mistakes, and wrong decisions, and now, I've made a strict decision to push forward even more and do greater deeds. It's mental, and it's action. Winning and being successful in this life is saying to yourself, *no matter what comes my way, I'm going to fulfill this promise, I'm going to achieve this goal.*

It's called "goal orientation," which is a concept developed by Educational Psychologist, J.A. Elson, and defined as "your attitude toward setting and achieving goals."[1] This is why it is imperative to stretch yourself, test yourself, and stop limiting yourself. Again, your attitude matters towards everything that you do. All of us have a comfort zone, and most of us are afraid to step outside of our normal activities and daily routines. But, when you think about it, our normal routines create boredom in our lives. If you never challenge yourself to do better, and if you never fully focus on a goal or take the necessary steps to grow in life, years will pass, and boredom and contentment will seep into your mindset, showing up in your everyday existence, and ruining what could potentially have been a life's blessing.

Progress happens when we leave our comfort levels. Erik Thomas's famous words are, "What is your why?" I love to hear Erik, "ET" Thomas ask this question because I know that this is one passionate man that inspires others to challenge themselves to succeed. When I first started listening to Erik Thomas, it made me think about the importance of *my why*. My goals and his encouragement to my life made me sit down and think about how I was going to excel to the next level in my life.

If you find your "why" in anything that you set out to do, it will help you see what needs to be done; if you need to make a change, it will help you face the facts and force you to accept, and acknowledge, that a change in your life must be done. This process will begin to assist in the removal of your current comfort state and cause you to challenge yourself to a greater you. It's time for us to stop acting like babies; grow up and reach higher! Get rid of old habits and get some new habits!

> "And be not conformed to this world: but be ye transformed by the renewing of your mind, that ye may prove what is that good, and acceptable, and perfect will of God."
> -Romans 12:2

The previous Scripture is stating that we are to be transformed from the inside out, and in this manner, we can begin to change how we think; and when we change how we think, then we will begin to change how we live. The good news is that when you begin to change how you live, then you can reach that lovely goal. Challenge yourself!

Anyone who has appeared to be a light to your life had to set the bar higher for themselves than what they probably believed they were capable of. Again, challenge yourself! For example, men (hypothetically speaking) you want to take this beautiful lady out on a date, who seemingly appears to be a little out of your league; you have been interested in her for a long time. It's been almost two years; she is still single, and you're still single. However, you have not made a move to introduce yourself to her yet. Every time you see her, you start glowing and smiling, and she gives you the same type of expressions. Now, how much more of a sign do you need? The lady is giving you an indication that she may be interested in you as well.

Now, more time has passed, and you still have not approached her. The opportunity will probably pass you by, and at some point in time, you will wonder about the future you could have had with this young lady, especially if she decides to date someone else, and you still have an interest in knowing her better. I will say this again, it's necessary to always challenge yourself! Your confidence must be built up and then respectfully approach the young lady. It's possible she has been waiting for you to show your interest. If you then set yourself to finally introduce yourself to her, and she refuses you at first, try again. If you later try again and she decides to go out with you, then you have successfully accomplished a goal. Now, if she had refused you again, I would say, just let it be. You let her be, and if she had come to you later, then I would say continue with your quest to get to know her better.

Now, back to my point. It is the same with your life's purpose, your dreams, and your goals. . . go for it. Aim for that which seems unobtainable. I'm using this example as an analogy, so you can be daring in your moves for being distinguished in your life's journey. I'm always going to shoot for the sun, the moon, *and* the stars; you have to believe in yourself and strive for all that God has purposed for you to be as well.

When you challenge yourself, mediocrity will become a thing of the past. You will begin to dismiss a normal lifestyle and mentality. In this process, a paradigm shift becomes present and real in your life. When your mindset is renewed, and you become more focused, firm, and reserved in your decision to achieve higher, then you will begin to notice that you are advancing. You will see how you are changing for the better. The key is having a vision and making a plan to achieve the goal.

The quality of anything will be low if there is no strong foundation! I'm giving you the basics, now, move on up, like "George and Weezy" on *The Jeffersons*. A path has already been designed for you; don't be lazy! Don't be alarmed! Surely, don't fear. There will be times when you feel hesitant and feel too tired for the challenge; do it anyway and then commit yourself to it.

God gives you strength! Isaiah 40:29 says, "He gives strength to the weary and increases the power of the weak" (NIV). He will give you anything you ask for, because whether you know this or not, it is God who promotes, and it is God who provides and gives you His grace to excel and prosper. If He does this for you, then why don't you act on the authority given you through Him and go beyond your own limits!

Succeed beyond others' expectations and opinions of you and then look at yourself in the mirror with a humble smile and say, "Look at Gawd (God)," or start rapping, "I'm bad," by LL Cool J. I challenge you to "Challenge you!"

## KEEP YA HEAD UP

*"So keep your head high, keep your chin up,
and most importantly, keep smiling, because life's
a beautiful thing and there's so much to smile about."*
-Marilyn Monroe

In this book, I wanted you all to see how reaching your goals is so important. There are many, many people who have made significant, complimentary, and outstanding transformations in their lives and have achieved enormous success in one way or the other. Remember, a goal does not always classify as a work or career endeavor. Reaching a goal describes anything that one ascribes to that will generate a successful completion, according to their desires and what's in their hearts. Some exhibit one, or all, of the attributes or qualities noted in this book that have produced a favorable outcome.

These individuals that I will acknowledge fought the good fight of faith, challenged themselves, and became victors. These jewels. . . well, they had a dream, achieved it, and made a difference in their lives and the lives of those who were watching them. Look around you; you are a star in someone's eyes. I know there is someone who has positively influenced your life, also. The Bible says in Hebrews 6:12 "That ye be not slothful, but followers of them who through faith and patience inherit the promises. (KJV).

## SCENARIOS OF VICTORS

I'm going to dedicate this brief chapter and the next to highlight certain individuals I believe deserve to be honored because they are Warriors. Each one of these individuals exemplifies champion status in their own right. They are winners, and I declare to you that you are a winner too!

These people who I will show adulation to deserve it. These went through hardships, probably lost their hope and faith; they probably experienced fear at a level unexplainable. These fighters probably lost everything they worked so hard for, and perhaps at one point in time, they wanted to give up on everything —probably feeling that what they were striving for wasn't worth the time. Some probably even thought that there was no way they would survive another day. Each one of these individuals I will speak about may have been faced with a life-threatening or a difficult challenge that was meant to destroy them, wipe them out, or keep them at a level in life, which seemed they would never defeat. But God! Don't ever give up trusting God!

These individuals did something powerful; they changed their mindsets to an "I can succeed" mindset. They knew who they were; they tapped into their inner strength and became "The Challenger" instead of being "the challenged." They visualized themselves reaching the goal, and then they made a vow to accomplish that goal. Day by day, they worked on a particular step toward the fulfillment of that goal, and they became determined. In the end, it was achieved! Done! Completed!

I'm pretty sure that even after the negative experience they encountered pushed them down temporarily and tried to keep them under, their faith increased, they had a higher level of appreciation, increased sensitivity to things, and a greater understanding of life. These individuals were likely filled with gratitude and compassion and abounding with so much more wisdom. I know that their relationship with God became much better, stronger, and more "lovingly intense."[1]

After their goal was accomplished, they were satisfied, merry, and joyful. They knew in their spirit that "all things are possible through God" (Mark 9:23), and that if they only believed, and apply themselves to a greater extent, that there was nothing they could not do. These are the people who determined that nothing or no one could stop them from having life and having it more abundantly. They were thankful! See, once you know that God has a specific purpose designed specifically for your life, then that's when you start the production process.

This is where I want you to be; you need to know, and you must believe, that you are significant, courageous, and needed by others. Know that whatever calling is on your life, when you apply every major point in this book, it lines up with God's will for your life, so there is no mountain that you cannot climb!

TESTIMONY OF A VICTOR

Some of the people who I believe have fought to overcome many challenges and are victors are:

> *You! Me!* Steve Harvey, Tyler Perry, Jim Carey, Oprah Winfrey, Walt Disney, Thomas Edison, Sidney Poitier, Winston Churchill...our grandparents and our great-grandparents who fought troubled waters growing up as kids. I mean, I can keep on with names of victors; what about Kenneth Hagin, Bill Gates, Nas, Tupac, Tiffany Haddish, Drake, Stevie Wonder, Mike Lindell (The Pillow Man), DNice...I can go on and on.

My spiritual leaders went from a season of lack to now having successful, Bible-teaching churches all over the world. So, you can prosper, you can accomplish anything, you can win at reaching any goal. You are a blessing to others; you are a blessing, period! Your life matters, and your goals matter!

> *"Even though you're fed up,*
> *you've got to keep your head up."*
> -Tupac

Now, I'm going to give you a miraculous case scenario of a person who has had major life challenges, maintained an "I will win, I will accomplish this goal" mentality, stayed focused, pressed through the pressure, believed in the power of God, and then slayed the goal, ultimately resulting in victory! I'm choosing this individual to talk about because I have seen her transformation, and I have seen what God can do, and how full of determination and drive was within her to overcome a major health issue. You know, without being completely healthy – with all major body faculties in working order – everything else in life is limited. Therefore, you must take care of yourself, making and maintaining your relationship with God and your health as the ultimate priorities.

My aunt, Marie Wilson, was born healthy, grew to love being pretty, dancing, and having a good time. She loved to party; that was her thing to do. She was a young mom, but she enjoyed her life, and she was full of joy. But, on April 5, 1984, on the day of her mother's birthday, my grandmother, and at the age of twenty-two, my aunt woke up and noticed she could not move and could not walk. After being rushed to the hospital, she was diagnosed with Multiple Sclerosis. My family went through the process of caring for my aunt daily. Remember, sickness, illnesses, and diseases are the worst. No one wants it, and when you're in that battle, all types of emotions hit you: anger, depression, fear, lack of enthusiasm, etc. Think of the shame a person feels when family or healthcare providers have to come and fully do all of the things a once-independent person could do.

So, days, weeks, and months went by, and my aunt had shown no progression with recovery. As a matter of fact, she was told that she would never be able to walk again. I mean, think about what her doctor's report had done to her mindset and self-esteem. However, there was this dance show that came on every day, in the local Detroit, Michigan area, called "The Scene," and eventually, the show's name changed to "The New Dance Show." Not only did my aunt love that show, but for the most part, everybody loved that show. It came on Monday through Friday at about 6:00 p.m.; this was the program where everybody learned all of the latest dance moves, or at least learned how to get better at dancing.

To make a long story short, remember, my aunt loved to dance; this program acted as motivation to her to walk and be able to dance again. While watching "The Scene," she said to herself, *I'm gonna dance again*, over and over as an affirmation. She meditated on it. She visualized herself going out again, and partying and dancing as she had done before the illness attacked her body. Though the family still did not see any progress in her health, each day in her room, while she was by herself, she was taking action towards learning how to use the members of her lower body again. Each evening, she remained focused and took small steps to move around, move her body, all while watching "The Scene." A year later, there was still no change in her health, but her faith didn't waver.

Two years later, in 1986, the family was doing regular things like cooking, laughing, talking, watching TV; to our surprise, my Aunt Marie walked out of her room with no help from a wheelchair, no help from a walker, and no assistance from the family. Everybody was filled with so much joy and laughter, crying with happiness for her recovery, thanking God for such a miracle. It was truly a blessed day. The happiest moments were that it was about the time "The Scene" came on, and of course, she broke out with a dance move and guess what? She had been dancing nonstop for years Here it is 2020, and with multiple sclerosis, being such an unpredictable illness, my aunt is still strong, though her mobility has been slightly affected.

In retrospect, she was told she would never walk again. Her tenacity and unwillingness to give up encouraged me to never give up on anything in life. As the saying goes, *anything worth having is worth fighting for*. She had a vision to walk again, and she challenged herself to prevail. She had a will to succeed, and most importantly, God had a greater plan for her life. Other family members and friends who watched her transformations have been nothing but inspired by her recovery and their faith increased because of how God turned things around in her favor; she impacted the lives of many others. In that season of her life, when she was not able to walk, faith, endurance, and strength were born in her spirit.

She gives God all of the glory and is ever ready to share her story with anyone. . .at any time.

Her testimony remains dear to me because she weathered the storm in order to accomplish a dream, a goal that was in her heart. She is living proof that God answers prayers and that miracles do happen, even when we lost sight of things. I used her and the others mentioned above as examples to encourage you to challenge yourself. It's important that you see that people go through life-changing events and can still come out on top. These are known to be results-driven people.

Again, my aunt was told by neurologists that she would never walk again; but she kept striving and kept fighting. If this story did not touch your soul, then just think about somebody who you admire. I'm sure they have been through the trenches at least once in their lifetime. It's important to press hard for the mark and laugh in the face of pain and adversity. Honestly, we develop character and courage when our persistence to win against the odds is challenged and fulfilled.

Whatever your situation may be, see opportunity in it! See the glass full, not half full, and certainly not empty. You are not defeated! You have to say this as long as God gives you breath in your body. Pursue your dream. Your reaction to anything should be to cultivate a meaningful life. Maintain the vision in your head, which will remind you that you will bloom and that you will rise. So, keep ya head up!

*"...God gives His hardest battles to His strongest soldiers"*
-Habeeb Akande

## WORK YOUR PRAYERS AND FAITH

*"Prayer and Faith both are invisible,
but, they make impossible things possible."*
-Unknown

"I hope this business deal closes." "I hope they accept my offer on this house." "I just want to get this job". . . and so on and so forth. These are just a couple of uncertainties we're frightened by and badger ourselves with when we believe for a major goal to manifest in our lives. God is just like us. He loves it when we communicate with Him. It doesn't matter how big or how small the thing is, God wants to be included in every aspect of our lives. All of our hopes, dreams, desires, goals, talents, gifts, and abilities are God-inspired. So, why not let Him in on what we want in life. Why not express our sincere emotions with Him?

You should have goals that are so big that you cannot see the end from the beginning. I know in the past, before I renewed my mind with respect to what I'm seeking to achieve in life, I didn't realize how important it was to pray. I didn't know how important it was to believe beyond my own capacity, and I didn't believe that I could really live a grandiose life. But, I will tell you, I realized something, I can't do anything without God leading me, guiding me, making my path clear and blessing my plans; whether you want to believe it or not, you can't either.

1 John 5:14 says, "And this is the confidence that we have in Him, that, if we ask anything according to His will, He heareth us." I referenced this Scripture because it tells you that you can be secure in talking to God. Talk to Him, ask Him, and let Him know how you feel by explaining your emotions to Him. You know how it is important for you to be true to yourself? Well, it's of the utmost importance for you to be sincere and true with God.

This Scripture is one to meditate on. As a matter of fact, this is a verse that I chose as a positive affirmation because it is confirmation that God knows what I want and will give to me and you, too. It implies that God does notice and observe requests that we offer up to Him – assuring us that we can rest in the knowledge that He will answer our prayers. So, for God to answer your prayer, your petitions, and to approve and bless your goals, these things have to line up with His Word and His Will for your life: stand in agreement with God and with those who support and believe in your journey. It's vitally important to go to God in prayer genuinely, sincerely, perseveringly, and in faith.

Prayer allows God to show you your life's work. If you do not know why you're here, even if you do know your purpose or the goals you're seeking, when you pray, God will show you your life's purpose. But, you have to have ears to hear His Word, a heart to receive it, and willingness to be obedient to carry out the plan. God will answer you if it's according to His will. If not, He will answer and show you why you should not take the route you're so eager to follow. God is so good, and He will structure and restructure your life if you invite Him in. God will produce excellent results in your life because He is the Creator, and He can create anything for you. God gives all of us the motivation and inspiration to dream and to achieve goals.

Think about it this way, every one of us has wanted to work on personal development. We all have had to overcome challenges, change certain self-behaviors, tried to reach many of our life's goals, and live out our dreams. But, in essence, these are hard to do, if you do not know what goal you're seeking and apply these "goal exercises" that I have laid out in this book. Also, I am expressing the fact that through prayer to God, and applying faith, God will release the fears, anxiety, limitations, and stagnations you may battle and give you the desires of your heart.

God's Word tells us in Matthew, chapter 11, to "Come unto me, all ye that labour and are heavy laden, and I will give you rest. Take my yoke upon you, and learn of me; for I am meek and lowly in heart: and ye shall find rest unto your souls. For my yoke is easy, and my burden is light" (v28-30).

Some people do not want to allow God into their lives, but He will set you on high, He will place you above the enemy and your haters, and He will surely put you in a position to dominate in any area you are called to work in. His Word says in Psalms 75 that promotion comes from Him (v6). If you are not disciplined, persistent, or confident, and you are weak in any area – and it's hindering you from accomplishing a thing – then my honest suggestion is that you go to God in prayer and wait on His guidance. He will announce to you things to come. He will tell you which way to go, who to meet, who not to be involved with; He will advise you when you should make a strategic move and when to be still. He will tell you contrary to what you are praying for as well.

Sometimes, you may not like the outcome, but if you're going to pray to God for instructions and decisions, then you have to learn to trust Him and trust His Word. You will know if what you have prayed for is not for you because you may incur problems or the goal you're seeking may fail. If you pray and nothing continues to go right after all of your attempts, then it may just be the timing is not right, and more preparation is needed. It may be that God is trying to fix certain character traits that you exhibit to get you ready for greatness.

In a way, prayer allows God to be your spiritual partner so that you are directed to the goal you're trying to achieve. It's God's power and ability that allows for anything to be manifested in the natural. So, pray! Trusting Him is to be considered as faith.

From my perspective, all of our goals have a beginning, middle, and end. The beginning is where prayer begins, when we know what goal we are aiming for and construction of the goal process. The middle is the waiting period and when the obstacles arrive. It is the process of the goal where you must utilize the "goal exercises" that I mention in this book, and it's also the period where you must offer praises to God, in advance, for a finished project. The middle is also where you will decide whether to finish or quit; this is when affliction, persecution, cares of this world, the lust of other things, and the deceitfulness of riches will pressure you to give up because you feel like you just can't take any more. You know the mixed feelings syndrome? This is where your faith is tested, and this faith is what is necessary to stay strong to see this thing through.

The end is where you have achieved the goal, and now it's time to go to God in prayer, with thankfulness and gratefulness for carrying out your plan to an expected end. Mark 11:23, a well-known faith Scripture, says, "For verily I say unto you, That whosoever shall say unto this mountain, Be thou removed, and be thou cast into the sea; and shall not doubt in his heart, but shall believe that those things which he saith shall come to pass; he shall have whatsoever he saith."

My Bishop always emphasizes that there are five elements of faith. They are: "Hearing the Word of God, Receiving the Word, Believing the Word, Speaking the Word, and Acting on the Word," and this is precisely what Mark 11:23 conveys. After you pray and apply these elements of faith without wavering, the things you pray for will come to pass. Nevertheless, I'm going to continue to stress to you, that in order to reach any goal, you have to do your part.

Dr. Bill Winston says, "Activate your faith 'cause prayer needs faith." Now, I'm saying to you, *birth your dream!*

I know some of you may say, "Well, that's easy to say, to just pray." Well, yes, it is easy to say, "Just pray, and when I pray, how do I know it's God?" The way that you hear from God is through prayer, and then recognizing His voice from your own voice, your spouse's voice, your kid's voice, or anybody else's voice. You will have an inclination in your spirit, your inner man, and you will feel a sense of peace, and you will hear a small still voice that speaks to you. God will send people along our paths to give us sound advice, and in some cases, we accept their words of wisdom, and in other cases, we reject the information. Weigh the options. God will give us many signs, whether we notice them or not. Some describe hearing from God as either "Women's intuition" or "male logic."

I saved this subject of prayer and faith for last because it is essential in every aspect of life. When you pray, believe that your prayers are answered. Let God show you through prayer how to pursue and accomplish your dreams and goals. Don't let your dreams go unfulfilled. You must allow God to work on you, and you help Him by working on you, too. Technically, God does not need your help, but with anything, you have to show initiative. Now, there are people who will say, "I built this business on my own," or "My college degree is the reason I'm this successful." "I didn't have to pray." Unfortunately, these individuals attribute their goal success to themselves and do not accredit any of their accomplishments to God.

We all have a role in meeting our goals and with everything that we do. But, without God, we are nothing and can do nothing. It is God who establishes plans, it is God who promotes, it is God who prospers, it is God who gives increase, and it is His grace that assists us. You are on the winning side. You will reach your life's goals. Use your gifts, talents, and abilities given you by God.

*"Commit thy works unto the Lord*
*and thy thoughts shall be established."*
-Proverbs 16:3

## ABOUT THE AUTHOR

Detroit, Michigan native Tamieka Lee (T. Lee for short) is fully dedicated to empowering others to plan for purpose-filled lives of success. Whether mentoring college-bound youth or coaching leaders in the development of next-level strategies, her unique approach inspires all to break free from limitations and overcome obstacles to experience life transformation and lasting success.

As an author, speaker, and empowerment coach well-versed in the art of persistence, Tamieka knows the pathway to destiny and readily leads others on a journey to achieving their wildest dreams.

*To book Tamieka for an upcoming event:*
info@tamiekalee.com | www.tamiekalee.com

# NOTES

## 2. ORIGINAL INDIVIDUAL

1. Lyrics from *Do What You Wanna Do* by the Dramatics

## 4. YOUR MIND IS A TERRIBLE THING TO WASTE

1. Financial Post, "How to Manage Your 40,000 Negative Thoughts A day and Keep Moving Forward." By Sarah Lambersky. Originally Published, October 16, 2013. www.FinancialPost.com.

## 7. YOU MUST LEARN

1. Chazz Palminteri, A Bronx Tale: The Original One Man Show

## 8. UNSWERVING DETERMINATION

1. www.inc.com; published, July 26, 2016

## 9. IRON SHARPENS IRON

1. Meg Jay; The Defining Decade; www.goodreads.com

NOTES

## 10. CHALLENGING YOU

1. Trainingindustry.com, Leader's Guide to Effective Dialogue, 2019

## 11. KEEP YA HEAD UP

1. Robert Burns and Religion, Walter McGinty, 2018 Social Science.

# ADDITIONAL READING

"The Complete Guide on How to Develop Focused Self Discipline." Adam Sicinski, IQMatrix, 2009.
   www.blog.iqmatrix.com/self-discipline

"7 Ways to Push Past Your Limits and Realize Your Goals-Do Something Cool." By Steven Bloom. Published, April 24, 2012.
   www.DoSomethingCool.net.

"Persistence-The Key to Success With Focus and Burning Desire." Experiments With Success, A Journey to Explore the Realms of Success! Raj Kapur. January 7, 2017.
   www.experimentswithsuccess.com.

www.ingramcontent.com/pod-product-compliance
Lightning Source LLC
Chambersburg PA
CBHW050656160426
43194CB00010B/1970